Ages 3+

WONDER MAGIC MATH FUN

Practice Workbook For Preschoolers

Vanishing Ink | Reusable in 15 minutes | Thick Paper

Includes penholder, gripper and refills

Wonder House

Note I:

Extra-thick paper, no curling, the product uses the groove design to constrain the user's writing habits, use the special faded stylus pen, the writing will disappear automatically after writing, the basic handwriting is gone, the front handwriting has disappeared, no need to wait, Reusable, environmentally friendly and energy efficient.

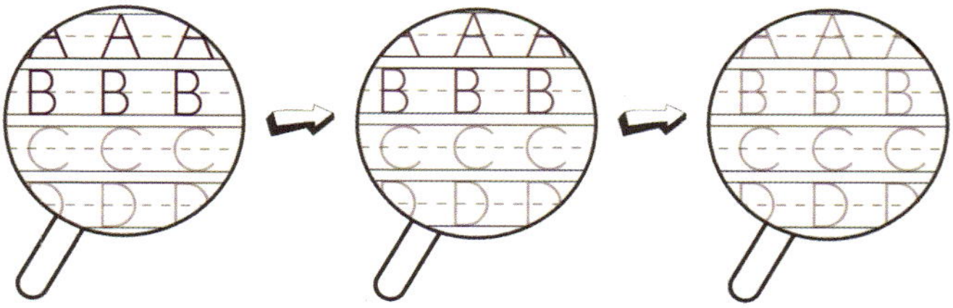

Note2:

This product is forbidden to wipe with force. Do not wipe with a damp cloth. Please keep it in a dry and ventilated place.

Note3:

1. Only use the special pen core for the product to write, the handwriting will disappear.
2. When the special pen core is in use, the ink may be clogged. Use the pen tip to lightly write several times on ordinary white paper, After the ink is smooth, then start the practice.
3. As the ink is specially processed, the handwriting will disappear after writing. Please do not use it for daily writing, record important information and sign documents, so as to avoid unnecessary losses to you.

Addition

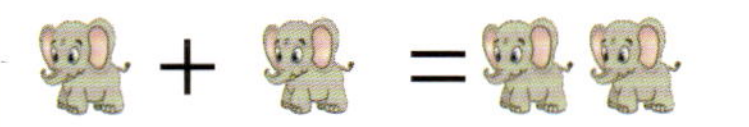			
1+1=2	1+1=2	1+2=3	1+2=3

1+3=4	1+3=4	1+4=5	1+4=5

2+2=4	2+2=4	2+3=5	2+3=5
		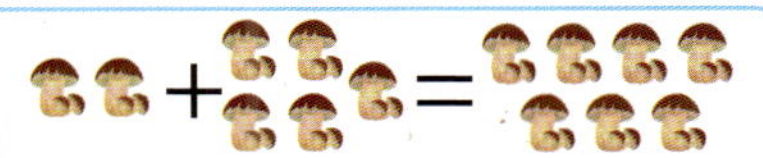	
2+4=6	2+4=6	2+5=7	2+5=7
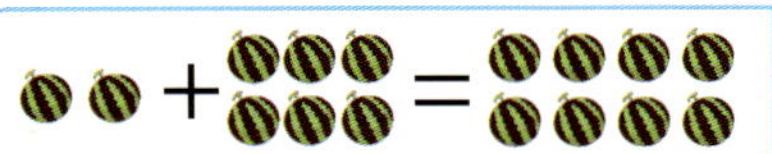			
2+6=8	2+6=8	2+7=9	2+7=9
		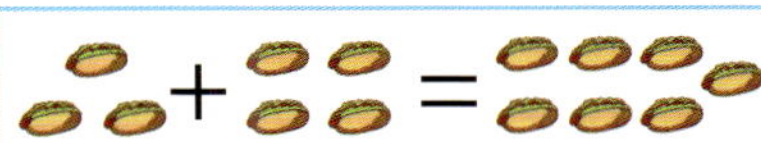	
3+3=6	3+3=6	3+4=7	3+4=7

Fill the blank

The two rows have hidden passwords. Using the number code find the passwords.

(1) 

____

(2) 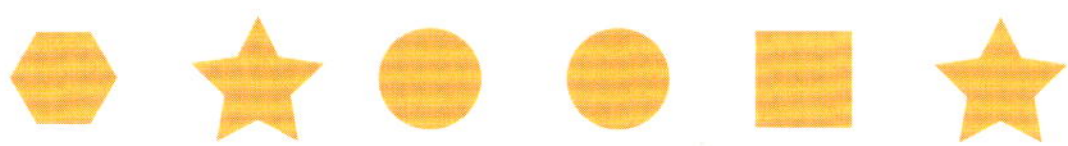

____

Look at the pictures and fill the grids.

9 - ☐ = ☐

☐ - 4 = ☐

☐ ☐ = ☐

☐ - ☐ = ☐

Subtraction

2-1=1	2-1=1	3-1=2	3-1=2

4-1=3	4-1=3	5-1=4	5-1=4

4-2=2	4-2=2	5-2=3	5-2=3

6-2=4	6-2=4	7-2=5	7-2=5

8-2=6	8-2=6	9-2=7	9-2=7

6-3=3	6-3=3	7-3=4	7-3=4

Fill the blank

Think and fill the grids.

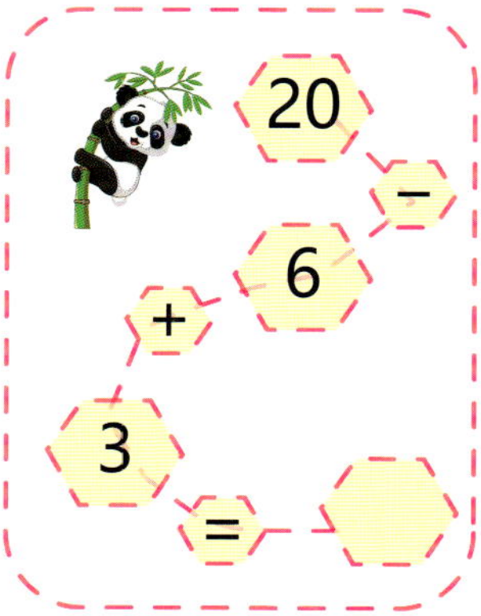

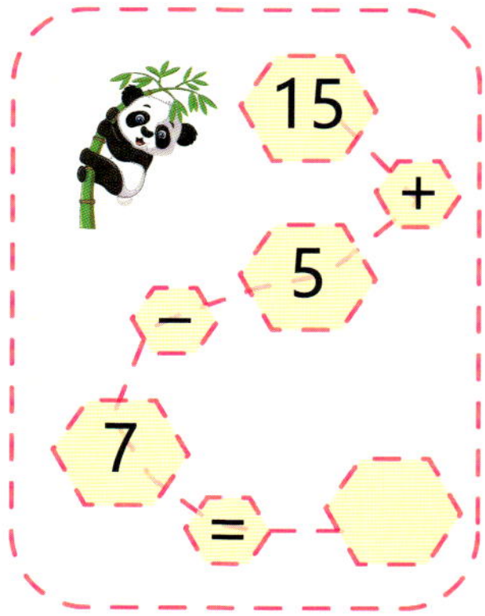

Solve the sums and choose the correct option.

6+5	1+10	2+3
9 10 11	10 11 12	5 6 7
2+8	**4+4**	**7+7**
9 10 11	8 9 10	12 13 14
7+6	**6+6**	**4+5**
11 12 13	11 12 13	9 10 11

Fun Math

1, 1 → 2	1, 2 → 3	1, 3 → 4
1+1=2	1+2=3	1+3=4
1, 4 → 5	1, 5 → 6	1, 6 → 7
1+4=5	1+5=6	1+6=7
1, 7 → 8	1, 8 → 9	1, 9 → 10
1+7=8	1+8=9	1+9=10
2, 2 → 4	2, 3 → 5	2, 4 → 6
2+2=4	2+3=5	2+4=6

Sum and difference

Count and help the kangaroo get the correct number or an orange.

 9+1

 10-2

 9-3

 5+5

 6+2

 2+4

Fill the grid and make each row and column equal to ten.

3	2	
	7	1
		4

5		1
		2
2		7

Fun Math

2 5
7
2+5=7

2 6
8
2+6=8

2 7
9
2+7=9

2 8
10
2+8=10

3 3
6
3+3=6

3 4
7
3+4=7

3 5
8
3+5=8

3 6
9
3+6=9

3 7
10
3+7=10

4 4
8
4+4=8

4 5
9
4+5=9

4 6
10
4+6=10

Subtraction

Subtraction means take away.

?				
Minuend	3	7	11	18
Subtrahend	1	5	6	9
Difference	( )	( )	( )	( )

Fill the ● and make each line equal to 15.

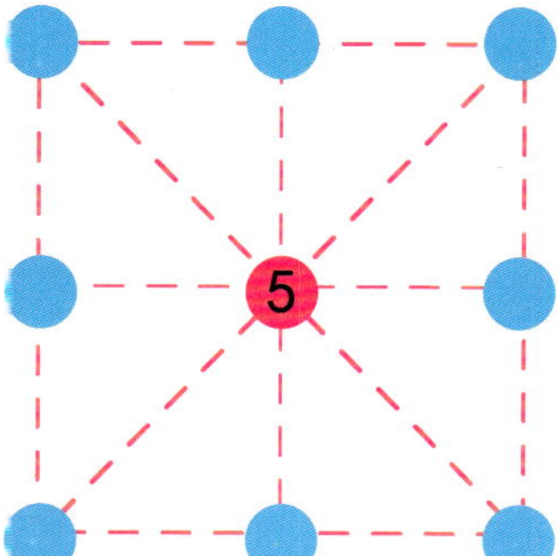

Fill the grids with the numbers below.

4 16 8 12

[ ] + [ ] = [ ]

[12] - [4] = [8]

[ ] + [ ] = [ ]

[ ] - [ ] = [ ]

Fun Math

2
1 1
2-1=1

3
1 2
3-1=2

4
1 3
4-1=3

5
1 4
5-1=4

6
1 5
6-1=5

7
1 6
7-1=6

8
1 7
8-1=7

9
1 8
9-1=8

10
1 9
10-1=9

4
2 2
4-2=2

5
2 3
5-2=3

6
2 4
6-2=4

Count and fill

Which is > or <?

5+9 ◯ 5+6

8+4 ◯ 8+9

15-7 ◯ 14-5

17-5 ◯ 16-3

Find a secret in addition.

6+7= ☐	2+8= ☐
3+6= ☐	5+5= ☐
6-5= ☐	8-4= ☐
9-3= ☐	5-2= ☐

Solve the equation.

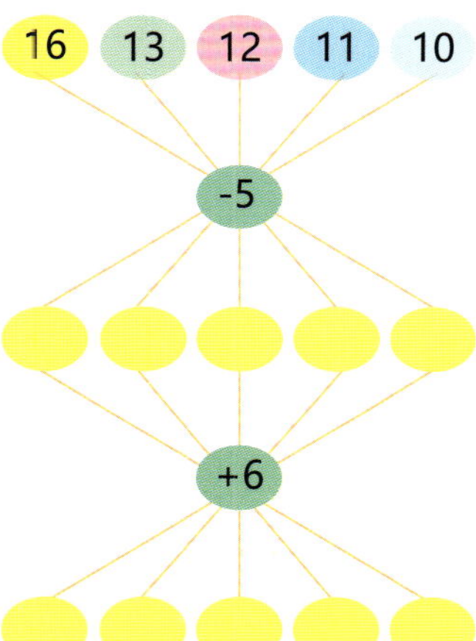

Find the regulation.

		6	8		12	
1	3		7			13
6		8	9		11	
21			15		11	
	18			12	10	
	7		11		15	

Fun Math

7	8	9
2 5	2 6	2 7
$7-2=5$	$8-2=6$	$9-2=7$

10	6	7
2 8	3 3	3 4
$10-2=8$	$6-3=3$	$7-3=4$

8	9	10
3 5	3 6	3 7
$8-3=5$	$9-3=6$	$10-3=7$

8	9	10
4 4	4 5	4 6
$8-4=4$	$9-4=5$	$10-4=6$

Counting basis

Which apple's sum is equal to 12?

Addition

1+1=2	2+1=3	1+3=4	1+4=5
1+5=6	1+6=7	1+7=8	1+8=9
1+9=10	2+2=4	2+3=5	2+4=6
2+5=7	2+6=8	2+7=9	2+8=10
2+9=11	3+3=6	3+4=7	3+5=8
3+6=9	3+7=10	3+8=11	3+9=12
4+4=8	4+5=9	4+6=10	4+7=11
4+8=12	4+9=13	5+5=10	5+6=11
5+7=12	5+8=13	5+9=14	6+6=12
6+7=13	6+8=14	6+9=15	7+7=14
7+8=15	7+9=16	8+8=16	8+9=17
9+9=18			

Number of days in a year

Number of days in a year		Number of days in a leap year
365		366
31	January	31
28	February	29
31	March	31
30	April	30
31	May	31
30	June	30
31	July	31
31	August	31
30	September	30
31	October	31
30	November	30
31	December	31

February in a leap year has 29 days.

Subtraction

1-1=0	2-1=1	2-2=0	3-1=2
3-2=1	3-3=0	4-1=3	4-2=2
4-3=1	5-1=4	5-2=3	5-3=2
5-4=1	6-1=5	6-2=4	6-3=3
6-4=2	6-5=1	7-1=6	7-2=5
7-3=4	7-4=3	7-5=2	7-6=1
8-1=7	8-2=6	8-3=5	8-4=4
8-5=3	8-6=2	8-7=1	9-1=8
9-2=7	9-3=6	9-4=5	9-5=4
9-6=3	9-7=2	9-8=1	10-1=9
10-2=8	10-3=7	10-4=6	10-5=5
10-6=4	10-7=3	10-8=2	10-9=1

Color by Number

Solve the sums and color the picture according to the color code.

RED: 1	WHITE: 3	BLACK: 4	YELLOW: 2

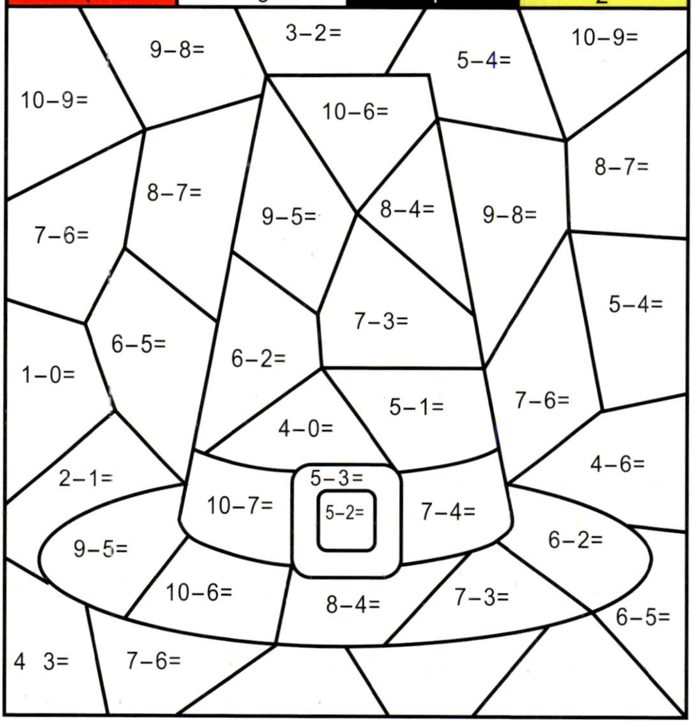

GOOD POSTURE

1. Both feet on the floor
2. Elbows off edge of desk
3. Sit back in the chair
4. Shoulders slightly forward
5. Proper desk height

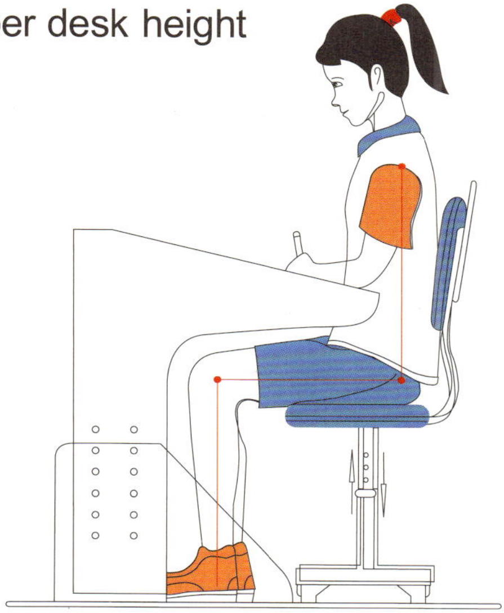

GOOD HANDWRITING

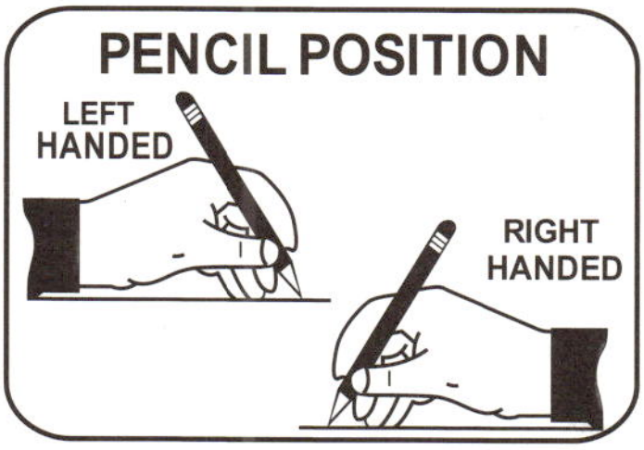

WONDER MAGIC MATH FUN

Practice Workbook For Preschoolers

Get ready to embark on a writing journey like no other! This interactive book for beginners with vanishing ink will inspire children to practice Math problems repeatedly. The book allows beginners to enhance their handwriting skills by following the grooves to solve Math problems accurately.

Let the interactive book guide you to write confidently and have fun!

Titles in the series

Wonder House

Wonder House Books is an imprint of Prakash Books

UK £ 1.99 CAN $ 4.99 US $ 2.99

ISBN: 978-93-6214-726-4

9 789362 147264

Wonder House

MRP

www.wonderhousebooks.com • 00005900

wonderhousebooks wonderhousebooks wonderhousebook